Hayling Island
in old picture postcards

by
Robert Godfrey

European Library – Zaltbommel/Netherlands

GB   ISBN 90 288 5290 5 / CIP

© 1991 European Library – Zaltbommel/Netherlands

INTRODUCTION

Hayling Island has always been a special place to visit for a picnic by the sea or a healthy holiday — it's still the south coast's 'paddler's paradise'. But this century has seen the erosion, with increasing speed, not only of the southern coastline, but also the island's rustic charm. Gone for ever are most of the tree-lined roads, thatched cottages and acres of green fields. In their place have come wider, straighter roads to accommodate the holiday and rush-hour traffic jams, high blocks of flats and housing estates.

The advent of the railway link with the mainland in 1867 — axed in 1963 — and the growing interest in 'seaside resorts' (sparked off by George IV the previous century) put Hayling firmly on the map for holidaymakers and daytrippers who readily streamed to the island's unspoilt six square miles on excursions by char-à-banc and train from London and all parts of Surrey, Berkshire, Hampshire and Sussex.

Until the road bridge was opened in 1824 the island was accessible only by ferries and a wadeway from Langstone. In stormy weather it was completely cut off.

One of the island's first developers, Lord of the Manor William Padwick, immediately embarked on several grandiose schemes to popularise Hayling as a seaside resort, on the lines of Brighton and Bognor Regis.

Still to be seen today is the ill-fated Norfolk Crescent, on the seafront, magnificent in concept but abandoned halfway through and destined never to be completed. Then came the Royal Hotel and the classical Bath House and library, later a café.

After these, Padwick ran out of steam but kept the courts busy with endless actions against his island tenants. The wealthy saw their opportunity to move in, buy cheap land and build themselves large impressive houses. The less well-off bought plots from farmers at the wilder eastern end of the island, erecting weekend shanties built around old railway carriages. Most of these have now gone, replaced by brick houses, flats and bungalows. With the upgrading of property Eastoke has become respectable, its old name of 'Bungalow Town' long forgotten.

The island has seen many development schemes appear and disappear over the years — among them proposals for a bridge to Portsmouth and the extension of the railway to the south-western shore, where a pier and dock were to be built in anticipation of vast business from cargo boats. Initial enthusiasm for steeplechase racing in front of the Royal Hotel failed to establish regular race meetings and the proposed annual season of regattas also failed to raise sufficient financial wind to keep them afloat.

Despite this lack of success as a super seaside resort the island has nevertheless expanded its population from about 2,000 at the turn of the century to some 18,000 today, as more people have chosen Hayling as their home.

Early observers maintained that by retaining its unspoilt natural advantages the island must steadily gain favour. But the speed of 'progress' accelerated and the need to provide housing for the thousands who work in Portsmouth, Havant and Chichester has regrettably obliterated many of the old-world charms of yesteryear, despite the best efforts of many residents who value such things. Planners always succeed in making the away-from-it-all places just like the places people are trying to get away from!

But Hayling Island still has its secret corners — like Tourner-bury Woods, believed to have been the site of a Roman hill camp. Legend has it that the island was named after the Saxon chieftain Haegel. Later, in 1043, the island was owned by Emma, wife of Ethelred the Unready, and later of Canute. She was the mother of Edward the Confessor.

In the middle ages the island was heavily forested and very much larger than it is today. Between 1294 and 1325, when the island's southern shore extended as far as the Nab Tower, some 300 acres of farmland were swept away by tidal inundations. With hundreds of acres of farmland went Hayling's first church which, some say, lies two miles out at Church Rocks in Hayling Bay.

Like all quiet sea coasts the island became the haunt of smugglers and wreckers, who were joined by deserters from the Navy and Portsmouth dockyard. They found the wastelands of Hayling a secure place to hide. The gang of smugglers became known as the Forty Thieves and there are many stories of encounters with the Revenue men. Gable Head is so named, it is said, because the gang tried to hang a man there who they believed had betrayed them. The Revenuers saved his life!

For the early inhabitants Hayling really was a land of milk and honey. They grew their own crops and vegetables, keeping cattle for milk and meat, chickens for eggs, bees for honey, and supplementing their diet by catching fish from the sea and shooting the abundant numbers of partridges, pheasants and rabbits.

The production of salt, carried on for some 1,000 years, was at one time a major trade with tons being taken by cart to the mainland every year. The island also exported large quantities of excellent oysters until the industry died after fears of pollution. One oyster bed became a swimming pool at a holiday camp, one of several established on the island in the 1930s.

The 19th century's new-fangled pastime of sea bathing or paddling seems to have done most to popularise Hayling as a resort. Noted for its bracing breezes, the island also offered one of the best stretches of sand on the south coast, uncluttered by other resorts' seaside paraphernalia. Hayling's reputation as a healthy resort, with long hours of sunshine, mild temperatures and balmy air, inspired the setting up of a TB hospital and convalescent home for cripples and feeble children. It was said in the 1920s that no doctor could afford to live on the island because the residents were so healthy!

Bathing machines, introduced a century ago to enable swimmers to change at the water's edge, can no longer be found but modest bathers can still use beach huts. Even as late as 1930 a local guidebook warned that 'it is laid down in the bye-laws of the local authority that bathing without a hut or an effective dressing screen is not permitted within 200 yards of any place to which the public have access.' Fifty years later astonished islanders were shocked to find nude bathers on their beach!

I would like to thank my many friends on Hayling Island who have helped me gather together this interesting collection of old photographs which so many more people will now be able to share.

The Sunny Sands. Hayling Island.

1. For generations Hayling Island's five miles of 'sunny sands' have been noted as a padler's paradise, ideal for children. The island's main claim has always been that its seafront remains largely unspoilt by modernisation into a man-made resort. Even today, with wide new roads and housing estates, the island's beaches are bounded by natural gorse-covered beachlands. The Victorian image of a paddling beach for mother and her children is just as true today.

2. The health-giving properties of sea bathing, coupled with Hayling Island's bracing air — 'purest of the pure, full of ozone,' said the early guidebooks — prompted convalescent homes to move to the island. The island's publicity claimed that bathing at Hayling could not be surpassed at any resort in the country or even on the French side of the Channel. Bathing machines and huts could be hired to preserve the modesty of bathers, while health freaks could indulge in hot sea baths at the bathing station.

3. Early swimming costumes for ladies revealed little and a dip in the briny meant no more than a paddle up to the knees.

4. The 19th century Palladian style library, built for the residents of Hayling at Beachlands, in front of Norfolk Crescent, later became a café to cater for the increasing numbers of day trippers coming by car and char-à-banc.

5. Green's café, Beachlands, where refreshments welcomed the many coach parties who came for a day out by the sea.

6. The Royal was the first hotel to be built on the island in the early 1800s, when plans were drawn up by Sir Richard Hotham, who had developed Bognor, to turn the island into a super seaside resort. The hotel had an unrivalled position facing the sea with views to the Isle of Wight.

7. Carriages from the Grand and Royal hotels await the arrival of train passengers at South Hayling Station in 1910.

8. The single-track 'crab and winkle' railway opened in 1867 and helped to popularise Hayling as a resort by bringing thousands of holidaymakers and trippers from London and all parts of the home counties. In 1878 a cheap day return excursion from London cost 11 shillings (55p) first class and five shillings (25p) third class. Station staff pose for a photograph in the early 1900s.

9. One of the 'Hayling Billy' locomotives pulling two passenger carriages across the wooden bridge spanning the sea between the island and Havant. It needed expensive maintenance and the line was axed in an economy drive in 1963.

10. A miniature railway on the seafront at Eastoke proved a big attraction for mums and dads as well as the kiddies.

THE SANDS, EASTOKE. 99

11. The wide expanse of sands at Eastoke in front of the old Nab Club were a popular spot for families.

The Beach, Hayling Island.

12. Hayling beach in 1909 — children played with bucket and spade just as they do today, but adults rarely shed their heavy clothes. If they did, they changed into voluminous costumes in the privacy of a hut or tent.

Beachlands Huts, Hayling Island.

13. Not a bikini in sight − the beach huts at Hayling in the early part of the century. Sunbathers even kept their trilby hats on!

14. One of Hayling's larger seafront houses, Dilkusha, covered in a winter sprinkling of snow.

15. Sinah Warren, a millionaire's home, at the western end of the island, which was destined to become a holiday camp in the 1930s.

SS.2   SILVER SANDS, HAYLING ISLAND

16. Silver Sands, Eastoke, one of several holiday camps established on Hayling Island to cater for the working classes.

17. As Hayling became more popular with visitors enterprising showmen opened sophisticated amusements like this timber and plaster rock 'monkey island' – complete with a colony of real monkeys, which caused consternation when they escaped and climbed into neighbouring gardens.

18. An aerial view of Beachlands, showing the monkey island (right), funfair and café. Many trees have been lost to development since these days.

The Common, Hayling Island

19. The motor car changed the scene at Beachlands, requiring the setting up of special areas for parking. Picnics on the grass became even more popular.

18.

CREEK ROAD,
HAYLING ISLAND

20. Creek Road, Eastoke, became the island's most popular entertainments centre, with shops and arcades opening especially for visitors in the summer. Almost anything could be bought to make the holidaymakers' stay a happy one.

21. One of the island's notable characters was Toby Lock, a tinker who had travelled widely and chose to settle in Mengham, in a wooden walled cottage known as the Black Hut. He bought and sold most things and his donkey cart was always loaded with pots, pans, rags and bones. He sold tobacco and sweets in his little shop, smoked herrings and acted as a general carrier. Before he died at the age of 77 in 1918, he ensured a place for himself in the island's legends by swallowing a live toad in the Rose in June.

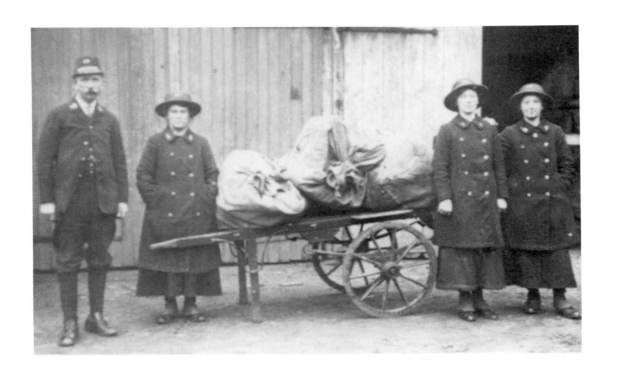

22. In the days of the penny post (halfpenny for postcards) this was the GPO's team on Hayling, seen with their mail-laden sacks on a handcart.

23. The **Mill Farm** dairy cart, pulled by Dobbin, made regular daily deliveries of milk throughout the island.

24. Horse-drawn carriages were the main form of transport on the island in the early part of the century. These residents were pictured on a Sunday afternoon drive.

The Crescent, Hayling Island.

25. Norfolk Crescent, a grand design for the seafront, was never completed. It was designed by architect Robert Abraham for his 'sincere friend', Lord of the Manor William Padwick, but abandoned when building reached halfway.

26. A modern 'Co-op' supermarket stands on the site of these old cottages at Gable Head.

The Pound, Manor Road, Hayling.

27. The Pound at Manor Road, where stray animals were kept.

Hayling Beach and Bathing Machines

28. The Bath House (left) on Hayling beach, where bathing machines were at the water's edge.

MENGHAM ROAD, SOUTH HAYLING.

29. Mengham Road, now a residential area and busy shopping centre.

Mengham Road, Hayling Island. 817.

30. Tree-lined and devoid of traffic — Mengham Road, when a man could peacefully smoke his pipe in the middle of the street, unworried by cars, double-decker buses and bustling shoppers.

Sea View Terrace. South Hayling. 5037.

31. Sea View Terrace in 1906. The low building behind the fence is Barber's bakery.

32. Railway porters pose for a picture with a bicycling friend in Station Road, West Town, by a newly thatched barn.

WEST TOWN . HAYLING ISLAND.

33. The West Town Hotel (right) still stands in Station Road, West Town, but other buildings have gone. The station taxi waits in the hotel forecourt beside a hand-operated Pratts petrol pump.

STOKE POST OFFICE, HAYLING ISLAND.

34. A pre-1900 view of Stoke, North Hayling, showing the post office on the left. The post-card was printed in Berlin.

35. Stoke, North Hayling, as it was in 1906: a new grocer's shop and a trim thatched cottage.

ELM GROVE, HAYLING ISLAND

36. Elm Grove, Hayling, now a busy shopping street, as it was in 1925 − just one motor car passes Elm Grove Free Church.

37. The Manor House, built in 1777 for the Duke of Norfolk on the site of an earlier building, the Grange. The manor house had a courtroom and the dovecotes, said to be the oldest in Britain, kept the household supplied with eggs and roasting fowl.

38. South Hayling's gothic Vicarage House, built for Reverend Charles Hardy, who became vicar in 1832 and was the first man on the island to wage war on the mosquitoes which bred in the saltmarshes and made life intolerable for many residents. He used to pay children a halfpenny for a dozen dead mosquitoes and handed out quinine to those affected by the bites.

39. Headmaster H.J. Earney of the primary school takes a class to see the breeding grounds of the mosquitoes in the 1920s.

40. Scientists from all over the world came to this house on Hayling seafront to visit the British Mosquito Control Institute, founded by J.F. Marshall in 1921. The house was known as Seacourt, the name later adopted by the tennis club built in the grounds, now known worldwide for its real tennis court and other racket sports.

41. Tournerbury, reputed to be the site of a Roman hill camp, is one of the oldest settled areas of Hayling and still the most rustic.

Northly Farm. N. Hayling

42. The island had many farms in its agricultural past. This was Northly Farm, North Hayling, in 1906.

43. The Rose in June, one of the island's popular public houses, in 1910.

44. An outstanding landmark, the water works tower built in 1895.

45. Meath House Hotel, Southwood Road, Eastoke, demolished in the 1960s to make way for an uninspiring estate of flat-roofed houses.

46. Ex-servicemen attend the laying of the foundation stone of the British Legion Hall at Gable Head.

Council Schools, Hayling Island.

47. The council school at Sunshine Corner, where children of all ages were taught until the opening of a comprehensive school in Church Road and primary schools in Mengham. Part dates back to 1876.

48. Monlas Place, North Hayling, destroyed by fire in 1921. It was formerly a vicarage for Reverend Matthew Monlas in the 17th century and was believed to have been built in 1486.

49. The Grand Hotel (left), now a school, and the Bungalow, which is incorporated into a funfair complex.

50. St. Peter's Church, North Hayling, and the old Vicarage House. The church was built in the Early English style in the 12th century and is the oldest on the island.

SOUTH HAYLING CHURCH.

South Hayling Church, Hayling Island.

51. Above: St. Mary's Church, South Hayling, dating from the 13th century, has a yew tree in the churchyard which some say is nearly 2,000 years old. It has a girth of more than 30ft.

Beneath: Interior of St. Mary's Church, little changed since this picture was produced in 1909.

52. The original Congregational Church building in South Hayling, destroyed by a German landmine in a 1941 air raid. A new church, now the United Reformed Church, was opened in 1954.

53. Sport has always been a popular pastime during the past century. This was Hayling Football Club's team in 1913.

54. Fish that didn't get away — George Spragg, who ran the Hayling ferry with his brother, proudly displays his big catch of tope and thornback skate.

THE CREEK, SOUTH HAYLING

55. One of the creeks at Mengham where, it was said, attempts were made to extract gold from seawater.

Hayling Lifeboat.

56. Above: The launch of Alderney's new lifeboat, the Proctor, in 1914 was attended by hundreds of spectators. The boat was named after an island family.

The Charlie and Adrian lifeboat which replaced Hayling's first lifeboat, the Olive Leaf, in 1888. The Charlie and Adrian was badly damaged in an embarrassing incident when it was launched from a new boathouse − the door was not tall enough and the boat's rudder was so badly damaged that the crew could not steer it. The inspector of lifeboats was among those who saw them flounder in the sea.

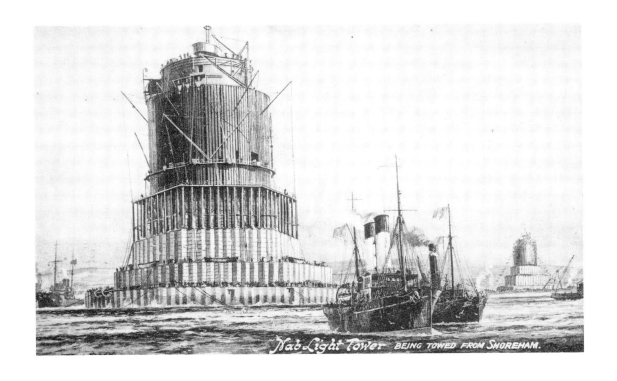

Nab Light Tower BEING TOWED FROM SHOREHAM.

57. The Nab light tower replaced a floating light off the south coast of Hayling in 1921. It was one of eight mystery towers built at Shoreham during the First World War; their purpose was never discovered. The cost of the tower, which consisted of 10,000 tons of reinforced concrete and 1,000 tons of steel, was estimated at a staggering £1,250,000.

58. Hayling's old, wooden toll bridge, opened on 8 September 1824, and replaced by a concrete structure on 10 September 1956, at a cost of £311,000. The old bridge, originally designed to carry horses and carts, was not strong enough for heavy vehicles — passengers had to walk when buses crossed. Repairs costing £100,000 were needed when it was decided to build a new bridge.

59. A tranquil scene at Bank Corner, Hayling — not a vehicle to be seen as these holidaymakers stroll in the sunshine of days past.

60. The wild expanse of common beside the seashore at South Hayling. On the left is Seager House, a boarding and day school for girls, run by the Misses D. and E. May. Their prospectus claimed that children were 'studied individually' and offered open air classes.

EASTOKE, HAYLING ISLAND

61. Eastoke Corner, a popular spot with trippers, as it was before the cafés and amusement arcades arrived to cater for visitors' needs. The open space in the foreground is now a car park.

62. One of the many leafy lanes that led to the sea at South Hayling in the early 1900s.

63. Shopkeepers in Station Road, Newtown, turn to stare at the photographer — an unusual sight in 1912.

Westfield Road, Hayling Island.

64. Cyclists pose for a picture in tree-lined Westfield Road, nearly ninety years ago.

Beach Road, Hayling Island.

65. Beach Road as it once was − but traffic is already increasing: note the old-fashioned bus and Austin 7, which have the road to themselves.

HAVANT ROAD, POUND CORNER, SOUTH HAYLING

66. Can this be Hayling's main Havant Road, so busy now with buses, lorries and traffic jams morning and evening? Only cart tracks mar the pristine carriageway.

67. Park Road, South Hayling, in 1906 — a gentleman in his cart clip-clops along a deserted highway.

MANOR ROAD, HAYLING ISLAND.

Manor Road: Hayling-Island

68. Above: One of the attractive thatched cottages which were so much a part of the Hayling scene in the early part of this century.

Beneath: A cart laden with hay in Hayling's Manor Road makes a picturesque postcard.

69. A busy day in Station Road, Hayling.

4325 BUNGALOW TOWN

PAN-AERO PICTURES.
KINGSTON-ON-THAMES

70. 'Bungalow Town', Eastoke, where trippers bought plots of land from farmers and built their weekend retreats. Many old railway carriages, costing only a few pounds, ended their days here and were gradually extended and improved.

71. Southwood Road, Eastoke, as it once was – holiday cottages created from old railway coaches.

The Beach - looking West, Hayling Island.

72. The unspoilt wildness of Hayling's seashore has attracted generations of families. Miles of sands are ideal for picnics and children's games.

73. The Victoria Hotel in Beach Road.

Mengham, Hayling Island.

3569

74. The hardware store remains on the corner at Mengham, but big new developments in recent years have turned the area into the island's main shopping centre.

The Sea Front, Hayling Island.

75. A grass tennis court at South Hayling, now obliterated by a block of flats.

Eastoke Beach, Hayling Island.

The Beach, Eastoke

76. Above: A view of Eastoke beach, where the sea frequently washed into the holiday homes built on the shingle. Piles of stones ended up in sitting rooms during strong gales and high tides.

Beneath: Visitors enjoying the wild expanse of beach at Eastoke, where sea defences were minimal and high tides often swept inland, washing away the shore.